THE
WATER CYCLE

Georgia Amson-Bradshaw

W
FRANKLIN WATTS
LONDON•SYDNEY

Franklin Watts

First published in Great Britain in 2017 by The Watts Publishing Group

Copyright © The Watts Publishing Group 2017

Produced for Franklin Watts by
White-Thomson Publishing Ltd
www.wtpub.co.uk
01273 479982

Series Editor: Izzi Howell
Series Designer: Rocket Design (East Anglia) Ltd

Illustrations from Shutterstock: Merkushev Vasiliy 5, Christian Mueller 5t, robert cicchetti 5b, peiyang 6, NKuvshinov 7b, Sentavio 8b, Sasha Fenix 9c, skelos 10b, wawritto 11t, LineTale 11bl, Galyna Andrushko 11br, studio23 12b, nadiya_sergey 13, Martchan 14l, Korionov 14c, Waddell Images 14r, Ziablik 15b, Jeff Gammons StormVisuals 15l, curiosity 16t, weily 16b, Suzanne Tucker 17t, Artisticco 17c, NASA images 19r, N-2-s 20c, ChiccoDodiFC 21l, Calin Tatu 21r, Dvolkovkir1980 21b, medesulda 22t, Crystal Eye Studio 22, poupine 23bl, Nucleartist 23br, Katvic 25, Armin Rose 26t, AridOcean 26b, Serjio74 27b, alphabe 28, Ciripasca 28b, Constantine Androsoff 29t, Nucleartist 29c, Arma banchang 29b

Illustrations by TechType: 17b, 18t, 18b, 19t, 19bl, 21t, 27t

All design elements from Shutterstock

ISBN 978 1 4451 5555 5

Printed in China

Franklin Watts
An imprint of
Hachette Children's Group
Part of The Watts Publishing Group
Carmelite House
50 Victoria Embankment
London EC4Y 0DZ

An Hachette UK Company
www.hachette.co.uk
www.franklinwatts.co.uk

Contents

What is the Water Cycle?

Water on Earth is being constantly recycled through a process called the water cycle. This is the movement of water between the Earth's oceans, atmosphere and land. It has four main stages: evaporation, condensation, precipitation and accumulation.

Evaporation

Water changes from its liquid state to a gas in this part of the water cycle. Water evaporates from the oceans, lakes, rivers and even plants, and becomes invisible water vapour in the air.

Condensation

Water vapour cools and changes from a gas into tiny liquid droplets in this stage of the water cycle. We see this happen in the formation of clouds.

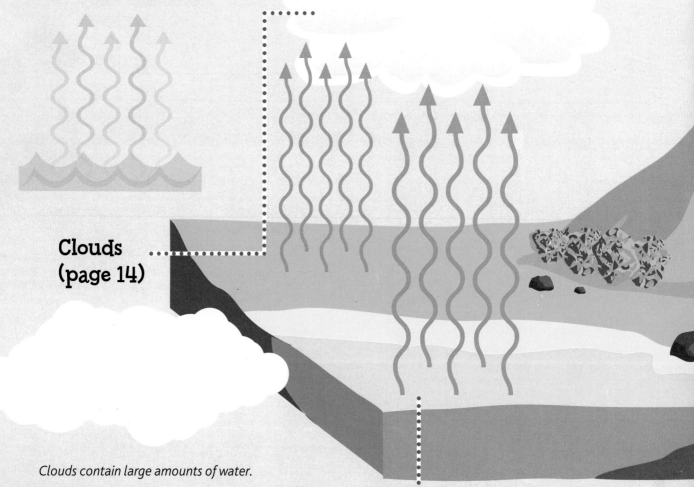

Evaporation (page 8)

Clouds (page 14)

Clouds contain large amounts of water.

Water stores (page 24)

Precipitation

As the tiny water droplets that make up clouds get bigger, they eventually become so heavy that they escape the cloud and fall as rain. If it's cold enough for the droplets to freeze, they fall as snow, sleet or hail.

Water drops fall as rain.

Rainfall (page 18)

Accumulation

Water that has fallen to the ground as rain, sleet, snow or hail soaks into the ground or runs over it. It gathers in water stores such as lakes or aquifers. No matter where it falls, it eventually makes its way back to the ocean, and begins the cycle again.

Water accumulates in rivers.

Transpiration (page 11)

River basins (page 22)

Our Blue Planet

Viewed from outer space, our planet is mostly a deep and dazzling blue. This is because 71 per cent of the Earth's surface is covered with water, most of which is salt water in the oceans.

Watery planet

Earth is the only planet in our solar system that has liquid water, due to its exact distance away from the Sun. If the Earth was closer to the Sun, it would be too hot and all the water would boil into gas. Further away from the Sun, it would be too cold and all the water would be frozen solid as ice.

Total volume

Although 71 per cent of the Earth's surface is covered in water, the total volume of water is tiny compared to the size of our planet overall.

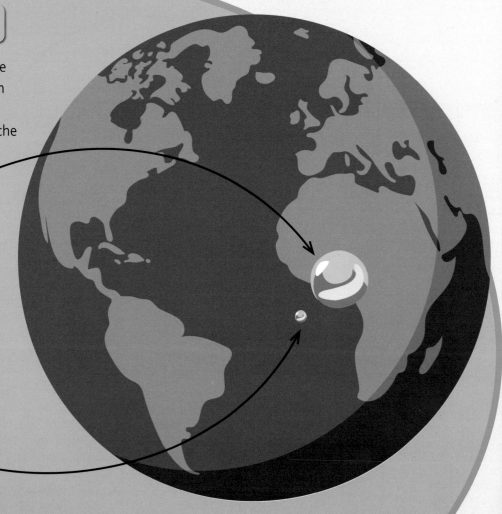

Salt water
This large drop shows how big all the salt water on Earth would be if gathered into a sphere.

Fresh water
The small drop here shows how big all the fresh water on Earth would be if it was gathered into a sphere!

Life

Water is essential for life on Earth. The very first living things on the planet evolved in the water in the oceans. Many creatures, including humans, rely on the fresh water in rivers, aquifers and lakes that is constantly replaced by the water cycle. We use fresh water to drink, wash and grow crops. Agriculture makes up the majority of our fresh water use worldwide. About 70 per cent of the water that humans take out of rivers and groundwater goes towards agriculture.

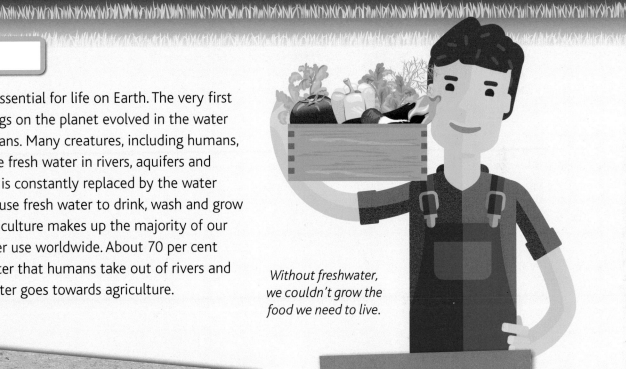

Without freshwater, we couldn't grow the food we need to live.

The water on Earth is constantly recycled: we don't lose or gain water from elsewhere in space. That means water you drank today is the same water that the very first living things swam around in!

FACT FILE

WHERE IS EARTH'S WATER FOUND?

96.5% is in the oceans (as salt water)

1.74% is in the ice caps and glaciers

1.7% is groundwater (in the ground)

The remaining 0.06% includes all the water that is stored in other places, including lakes, rivers, swamps, in the atmosphere and 'biological water' inside plants and animals!

Evaporation

Water on Earth is warmed by the heat of the Sun. This causes water to rise into the air as water vapour, in a process known as evaporation. Water vapour is an invisible gas that mixes with the air.

Oceans

Most evaporation, around 80 per cent, takes place from the oceans. This is due to the large surface area of the Earth's oceans, which provides the opportunity for large-scale evaporation to occur.

In balance

Globally, the amount of water evaporating is equal to the amount falling back to Earth as precipitation. However, the rate of evaporation versus precipitation varies geographically. More water evaporates from the ocean than falls directly back as precipitation. Meanwhile, more water falls as precipitation over land than evaporates into the atmosphere from the land.

Heat from the Sun evaporates water from the ocean.

Living things

Animals and plants give off water vapour into the atmosphere. Water vapour released by plants is called transpiration (see page 11). Humans put water vapour into the air by sweating and breathing.

Each person breathes an average of

400 ml

of water vapour into the air per day.

Sun power

The water cycle is driven by the Sun. Energy from the Sun heats water on the surface of the Earth. This causes liquid water molecules to break away as vapour and rise into the atmosphere.

A tiny amount of water vapour gets into the atmosphere through sublimation. This is where water molecules in ice break away into the air and become water vapour without going through the liquid state first. This is what makes it possible to dry your laundry outside even when it's freezing!

Humidity

There is always some water vapour in the air. Warm air can hold more water than cold air. The amount of water vapour in the air is called humidity. Because the amount of water the air can hold changes with the temperature, we measure relative humidity in percentages. 100 per cent humidity is when the air cannot hold any more water.

Hygrometer

Water vapour is an invisible gas, so it cannot be seen in the air. Even at 100 per cent relative humidity the air still appears clear. Humidity can be measured with an instrument called a hygrometer.

Hygrometers have a dial from 0 to 100.

Using evaporation

In hot countries, evaporation is used to harvest salt from the sea. Large flat pools of seawater are evaporated, leaving the salt behind which is then gathered up and sold.

The Amazon Rainforest

About ten per cent of the water vapour in the Earth's atmosphere is released by plants through transpiration. Transpiration is the process by which water is sucked up by a plant's roots, and given off as water vapour through holes in its leaves. The majority of the water in the atmosphere above the Amazon Rainforest comes from transpiration.

Amazon Rainforest

The Amazon Rainforest covers
40 per cent
of South America.

Rain source

Rainforests produce much of their own rain through transpiration. About 50 per cent of the water that falls as rain on the Amazon Rainforest was transpired into the air by the vegetation.

Plant types

Different plants transpire different amounts of water. A canopy tree in the Amazon transpires about 760 litres of water each year, whereas a large oak tree in a temperate region can transpire 151,000 litres over one year. 4,000 square metres of corn (roughly half the size of a football pitch) give off about 11,400–15,100 litres of water every single day.

The canopy is the main layer of treetops in the rainforest. Trees that poke through the canopy are called emergent trees. Trees in the main layer are called canopy trees.

Transpiration process

Steps 1 to 3 show how water moves through the plant during transpiration.

2: Stem
Inside a plant's stem are tiny 'tubes' that connect the roots to the leaves. Water absorbed by the roots travels up these tubes.

1: Roots
Water that has fallen to the ground as rain and soaked into the soil is absorbed by little hairs on the plant's roots.

3: Leaves
Plant leaves have tiny holes called stomata. Water that has travelled up the plant's stem is released as water vapour into the air through these tiny holes.

Microscopic close-up of a stoma in a tomato plant leaf.

Weather

Rates of transpiration in the Amazon and elsewhere are affected by the weather. During warm, sunny weather with high air temperatures, transpiration increases. During rainy weather, it decreases. However, when the air is very humid, as it often is in the Amazon, transpiration rates fall, as the air is already saturated with water.

The air in the Amazon Rainforest is always very humid due to the large numbers of plants transpiring.

Condensation

Water vapour that has evaporated from the oceans or land, or transpired from plants, rises up into the atmosphere. Higher up, the air is cooler, and water vapour condenses into small droplets of liquid water.

Atmosphere

The further up in the atmosphere you go, the colder the air is. Water condenses into clouds in the lowest layer of the atmosphere. There are no clouds in the higher layers of the atmosphere. This is because water vapour from the Earth condenses into clouds and falls as rain before it reaches the higher layers.

Droplets

The tiny droplets of liquid water that first form when water vapour cools in the atmosphere are very small; too small to be seen by the naked eye. It is only once droplets have joined together into much larger droplets and grouped together as a cloud that we can see them.

Cloud nuclei

Water vapour cannot condense into water droplets without having a surface to stick to. In the atmosphere, this occurs in the form of microscopic particles of dust or smoke that are also in the air. These extremely tiny dust particles are called cloud condensation nuclei.

Clouds forming in the atmosphere, as seen from space.

Cloud saturation

Eventually the droplets in the cloud get bigger and heavier to the point that the cloud becomes saturated. It then cannot hold any more water, and water drops begin to fall as rain.

Cold surfaces

You can see condensation in action around you every day. Condensation forms on the side of cold drinks and on people's glasses when they come in from the cold into a warm room. You can also see condensation if you breathe on a cold windowpane.

Dew

Water vapour in the air doesn't only condense high in the sky. During the night, the air temperature at ground level drops and the air is less able to hold water that evaporated during the day. The water condenses on the ground as dew. The temperature at which water vapour in the air begins to condense into dew is called the dew point.

Atmospheric storage

There is water in the Earth's atmosphere all the time, but it is only a tiny percentage of all the water on Earth. Scientists estimate about there are roughly 12,900 cubic km of water in the atmosphere at any one time. If all that atmospheric water rained at once, it would cover the Earth with a layer of water only 2.5 cm deep.

2.5 cm
2 cm
1 cm

Contrails

Another source of condensation in the air is aeroplanes. The engine exhausts from planes flying at high altitude contain water vapour. This condenses into the long cloud-like trails called contrails.

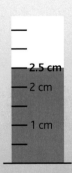

Clouds

Clouds come in many different shapes and sizes. Different types of clouds form at different altitudes. All clouds are made of condensed water in the atmosphere, but not all of them will go on to produce rain.

Types of clouds

Clouds are classified according to their shape and height in the sky. There are three main shapes – cirrus, cumulus and stratus, but there are many variations on these basic types.

cirrus

cumulus

stratus

Cirrus

Cirrus clouds form very high in the sky. They are thin and wispy. The word 'cirrus' comes from Latin, and means 'lock of hair' because that is what they look like. Cirrus clouds do not produce rain.

Cumulus

Cumulus clouds form quite low down in the atmosphere. They are fluffy clouds that look like cotton wool. They normally appear during good weather, though if they get big enough, they sometimes produce showers.

Stratus

Stratus clouds are low-lying blankets of cloud that cover the sky. They sometimes produce drizzle or snow if it is cold. They are the clouds that create a typical grey, cloudy day.

Clouds are very heavy! An average-sized cloud (which is about 1 km cubed) weighs the same as 100 elephants!

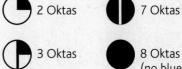

x 100

Cumulonimbus are storm clouds. They are huge and heavy, with a flat base and big fluffy plumes or peaks above. They produce extreme weather such as torrential rain and lightning.

Cloud cover

The amount of cloud cover in the sky is measured in oktas (which is the Greek word for 'eight'). This is an estimate of how many eighths of the sky are covered in cloud. Zero oktas is a completely clear sky, eight oktas is completely covered by cloud. The okta measurement is represented by these symbols.

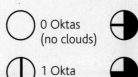

○ 0 Oktas (no clouds)   ◑ 5 Oktas

◐ 1 Okta   ◕ 6 Oktas

◔ 2 Oktas   ◑ 7 Oktas

◕ 3 Oktas   ● 8 Oktas (no blue sky)

◐ 4 Oktas   ⊗ Sky obscured

Reflection

Clouds act as insulation for the Earth, keeping it at a stable temperature. They can both reflect heat from the Sun away from Earth, or stop the Earth's heat from escaping into space, depending on the type of cloud and the time of day.

Precipitation

The most common type of precipitation is rain, which is water vapour that has condensed into large liquid drops. Snow, sleet and hail are also types of precipitation. They are formed when the air temperature is cold enough to freeze water droplets.

Rain

Water in the air becomes rain when cloud droplets collide and group into larger drops. The drops get bigger and heavier and eventually fall to the ground as rain (see page 18).

An area in Antarctica called the Dry Valleys has not received any precipitation for two million years.

Snow

When the air temperature drops below freezing, tiny ice crystals start to form in the air. Like the tiny water droplets that group together to become raindrops, these tiny ice crystals stick together and become snowflakes. Eventually they will be heavy enough to fall to the ground.

Snowflakes always have **six** sides.

Hail

Unlike snow which is made of many small ice crystals stuck together, hail is large pellets of solid ice that form inside a cumulonimbus cloud. They start as small ice crystals that get swept upwards in updraughts inside the cloud. They gather water on their surfaces which also freezes, making them grow. Eventually they become so heavy that they fall to the ground.

Some hailstones can get as big as golf balls, and can cause damage to people's property!

Climate change

Global patterns of precipitation are changing due to climate change. This means some areas of the world are flooding more often, and other areas are suffering from drought.

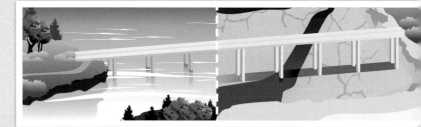

Uneven rainfall

Precipitation does not fall in equal amounts around the world. Some countries get much more rain and snowfall than others. The areas of the globe with the most rainfall are in the tropics, the areas near to the equator. This is because the heat from the Sun creates more evaporation in these regions. The hot, moisture-filled air then rises, cools, and drops the water again as rain.

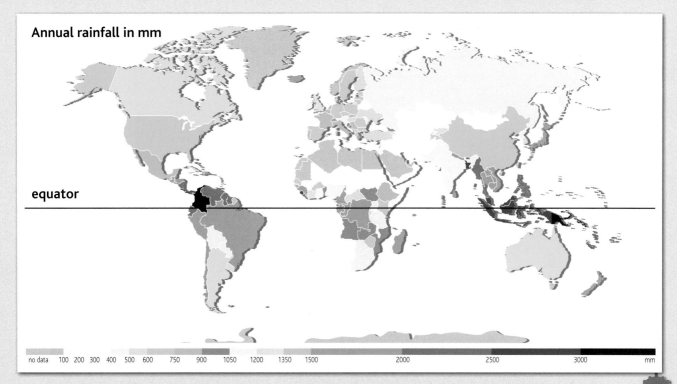

Annual rainfall in mm

equator

| no data | 100 | 200 | 300 | 400 | 500 | 600 | 750 | 900 | 1050 | 1200 | 1350 | 1500 | 2000 | 2500 | 3000 | mm |

Rainfall

Rain can be a light drizzle to an intense downpour. Rainfall is classed into different types depending on how it has been caused. Types of rainfall include convectional rainfall, frontal rainfall and relief rainfall.

Convectional rainfall

Summer thunderstorms are usually caused by convectional rainfall, which is driven by the heat of the Sun. This sort of rainfall is also common in the tropics, where the Sun is strongest.

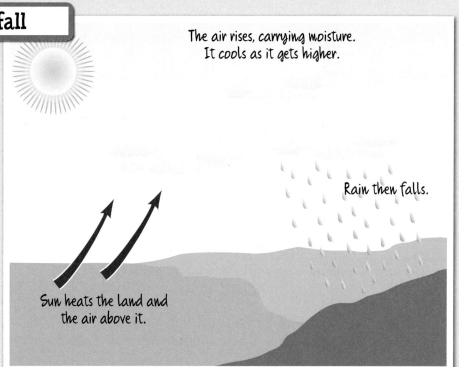

The air rises, carrying moisture. It cools as it gets higher.

Rain then falls.

Sun heats the land and the air above it.

Frontal rainfall

Air is moving around the Earth all the time. When a warm body of air meets a cold body of air, this meeting is called a front. The warm air will then rise above the cold air, itself cooling as it rises. As it cools, it drops any moisture as rain.

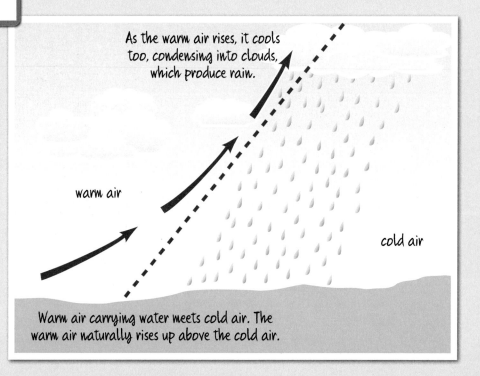

As the warm air rises, it cools too, condensing into clouds, which produce rain.

warm air

cold air

Warm air carrying water meets cold air. The warm air naturally rises up above the cold air.

FOCUS ON Rain in the Himalayas

The Himalayan mountain range in Asia is the tallest mountain range on Earth. It forms a huge arc about 2,500 km long from west to east. On the south-east side of the Himalayas are subtropical forests that receive a lot of rainfall. On the northern side is the dry Tibetan Plateau. This is because of a process called relief rainfall.

Relief rainfall

Hilly and mountainous places get a type of rainfall called relief rainfall. This rain is caused by moist air being forced upwards over higher ground, cooling the air and producing rain.

Warm air carrying water is forced to rise as it reaches a hill.

As it rises, it cools, forming clouds which drop the water as rain.

The air that passes over the other side of the hill has lost most of its water, and so that side of the hill gets very little rain. This dry area is called a rain shadow.

Bay of Bengal

Winds carrying moisture sweep in from the Bay of Bengal to the eastern Himalayas, where the process of relief rainfall causes all the water to be dropped on one side of the mountain range.

Rain shadows

Once the winds from the south east have dropped the moisture on the south-east side of the mountain range, there is no water left to fall on the Tibetan plateau on the northern side. This rain shadow means the Tibetan Plateau is very dry.

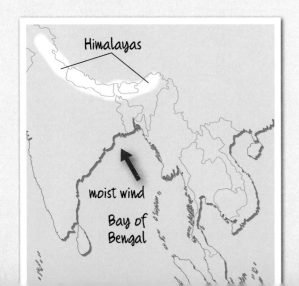

Himalayas

moist wind

Bay of Bengal

This satellite photo shows the rain shadow caused by the Himalayan mountain range. All the rain falls on one side of the range making it green and lush. The other side is dry and brown.

Accumulation

The final stage of the water cycle is the accumulation stage. Precipitation that has fallen to Earth travels over the ground or soaks into it. It gathers in water stores such as lakes, or moves to rivers where it flows to the biggest water store: the oceans.

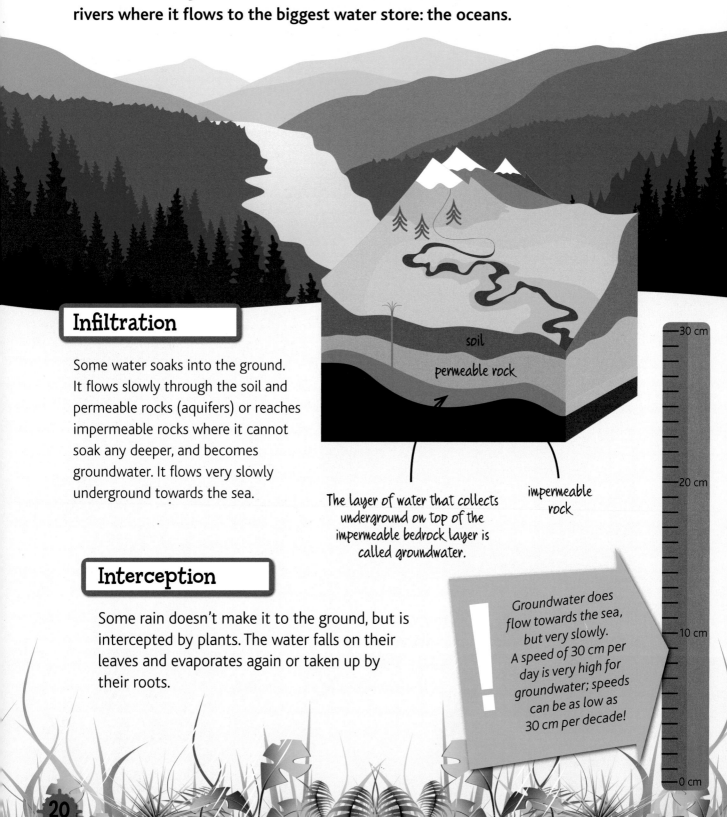

soil

permeable rock

impermeable rock

Infiltration

Some water soaks into the ground. It flows slowly through the soil and permeable rocks (aquifers) or reaches impermeable rocks where it cannot soak any deeper, and becomes groundwater. It flows very slowly underground towards the sea.

The layer of water that collects underground on top of the impermeable bedrock layer is called groundwater.

Interception

Some rain doesn't make it to the ground, but is intercepted by plants. The water falls on their leaves and evaporates again or taken up by their roots.

Groundwater does flow towards the sea, but very slowly. A speed of 30 cm per day is very high for groundwater; speeds can be as low as 30 cm per decade!

30 cm

20 cm

10 cm

0 cm

Surface runoff

Some water runs over the surface of the ground, and moves quickly to the rivers and into the ocean. This is called surface runoff. In places where the ground is either already saturated with water or is not permeable, there is a lot of surface runoff. In places where the ground is more permeable, there is less surface runoff.

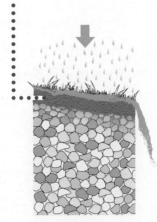

Rain falling on dry, permeable soil soaks into the ground.

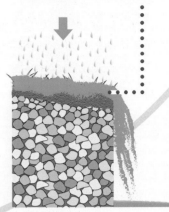

Rain falling on saturated soil cannot soak in and runs over the surface of the ground.

Dry soil

Saturated soil

Flooding

In cities, the ground is mostly covered by concrete or tarmac, so drainage systems are needed to carry away rain and prevent flooding. However, when too much rain falls in a short space of time the drains cannot carry all the water away, causing floods.

The city of Georgetown, Malaysia, during a flood.

Flooding is not just a risk in cities. Where the soil has been baked hard by the Sun, water cannot soak in fast enough, and so large amounts of runoff create a flood.

Water stores

Water that has fallen as many individual raindrops collects together into larger bodies again in the accumulation stage. These places where water gathers, or 'accumulates', are called water stores and include bodies such as ponds, lakes, rivers and the oceans.

River Basins

One of the main ways that rain that has fallen on the land makes its way to the sea is through streams and rivers. An area of land that is drained by a river is called a river basin.

Area

River basins vary massively in size, from millions of square kilometres (such as the Amazon river basin) to mere hundreds of square kilometres (such as Ombla river in Croatia, shown here).

Watershed

The edges of a river basin are called the watershed. This marks the highest point around the edge of the river's catchment area. Rain that falls outside the watershed will flow in a different direction, into a neighbouring river basin.

Tributaries

Rain falls onto the ground, then collects into small streams high up. These small streams merge together into a larger stack of streams and eventually rivers. The smaller streams and rivers that feed into a large river are called tributaries.

Mouth

The end of the river, where the water flows into the sea, is called the 'mouth'.

Gravity

Water always flows downhill due to gravity. This causes it to collect in valleys and depressions on the ground, which form streams, and eventually, rivers.

The Mississippi River

The Mississippi River is the main river in the largest drainage system in North America. Its tributaries include other major rivers, including the Missouri River.

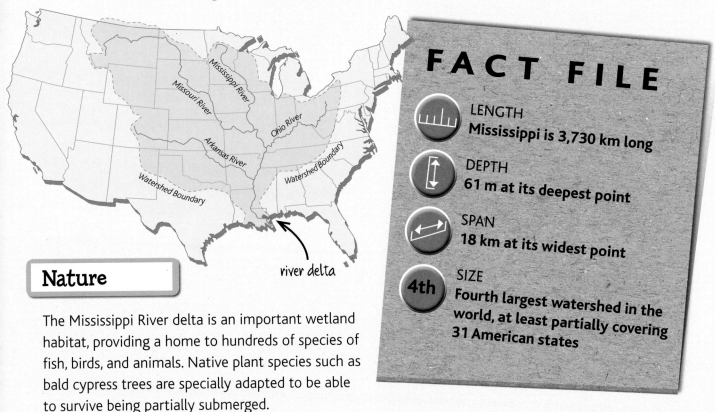

Mississippi River
Missouri River
Ohio River
Arkansas River
Watershed Boundary
Watershed Boundary

river delta

FACT FILE

LENGTH
Mississippi is 3,730 km long

DEPTH
61 m at its deepest point

SPAN
18 km at its widest point

4th **SIZE**
Fourth largest watershed in the world, at least partially covering 31 American states

Nature

The Mississippi River delta is an important wetland habitat, providing a home to hundreds of species of fish, birds, and animals. Native plant species such as bald cypress trees are specially adapted to be able to survive being partially submerged.

Humans

There is evidence that humans have used the Mississippi River for over 5,000 years. It is still very important to people today as a water supply and for shipping.

Climate change

The delicate wetland habitat of the Mississippi delta is vulnerable to climate change. Large storms, as well as sea level rises due to melting ice caps, damage the carefully balanced ecosystem.

Water Stores

While moving through the water cycle, water will be 'stored' in one place for a period of time, for example in a lake, a glacier or in the ocean. These places are called water stores.

Fresh and salt water

Most water is stored as salt water in the oceans. Only about 3 per cent of stored water is fresh, in both liquid and ice form. When water evaporates from the ocean it leaves the salt behind. That is why rain is made of fresh water, and lakes and rivers filled by rain are also fresh water.

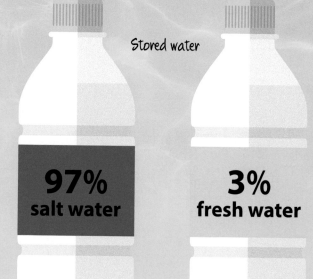

Stored water

97%
salt water

3%
fresh water

Surface water

Surface water is the name given to lakes, ponds, rivers and swamps. Although these kinds of fresh water stores are very important to humans, only a tiny 0.3 per cent of the Earth's fresh water is surface water! Most fresh water is instead stored in the form of ice caps and groundwater.

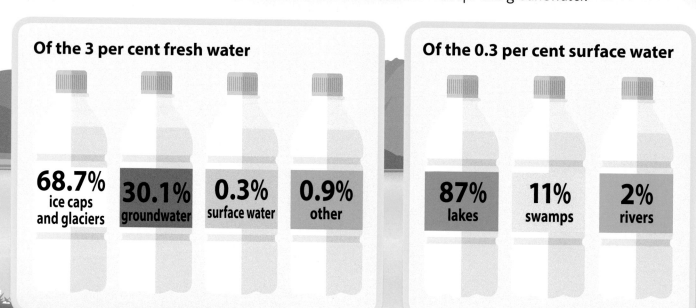

Of the 3 per cent fresh water

68.7%
ice caps and glaciers

30.1%
groundwater

0.3%
surface water

0.9%
other

Of the 0.3 per cent surface water

87%
lakes

11%
swamps

2%
rivers

Water in living things

Human beings are around 60 per cent water, and trees are around 50 per cent water. This sounds like it ought to make a lot of water overall, but in fact only a tiny 0.0001 per cent of all water on Earth is stored inside living things!

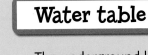 The largest lake in the world by volume of water is Lake Baikal in Russia. It is the world's deepest lake at 1,642 m deep. It contains 20 per cent of the world's unfrozen fresh surface water!

Water table

The underground layer of water called groundwater (see page 20) is one of the largest water stores. The top level of this layer of water is called the water table. Just like the level of water in a river or lake can go up or down, the water table can be higher or lower, depending on how much rain has fallen recently.

Ice caps and glaciers

Over two-thirds of the fresh water in the world is stored in the form of ice, in glaciers and as ice caps at the poles.

Polar Ice Caps

The polar ice caps are large sheets of ice up to 3 km thick that cover the land around the poles, in Antarctica and Greenland. Frozen water at the ice caps can stay stored there for thousands of years.

Formation

Ice caps form as snow falls onto land. The snow falls faster than it melts, so over time the weight of the snow on top compresses the snow beneath into clear ice.

Floating pieces of sea ice

North Pole

There is no land at the North Pole, so there is no ice cap. Instead there is a floating layer of sea ice that grows and shrinks with the seasons.

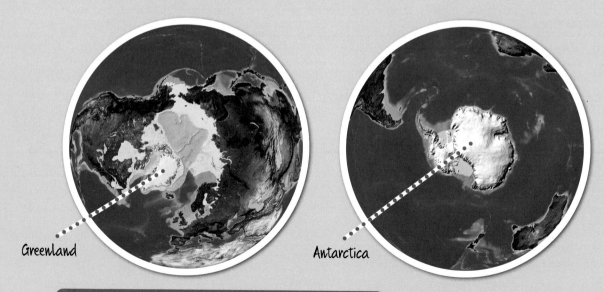

Greenland

Antarctica

Antarctica and Greenland

The two polar ice caps exist on the landmasses of Antarctica and Greenland. Nearly 90 per cent of Earth's ice is in Antarctica. 10 per cent is on Greenland. The ice on Greenland is so heavy, that the land below it has been pressed into the shape of a bowl.

Water level

Ice in glaciers and the ice caps plays an important part in keeping our sea levels stable. During the last ice age, when more water was locked up as ice, the sea level was 122 m below what it is now.

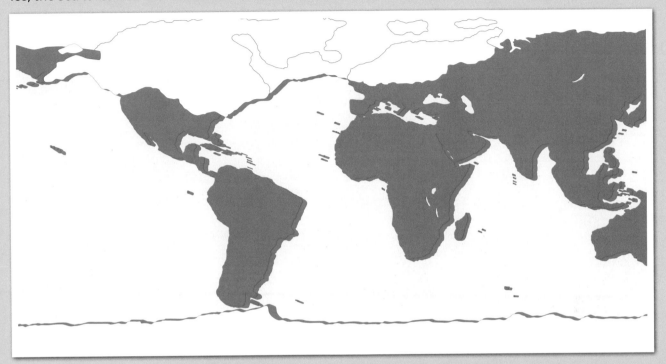

Lower sea levels change the shape of coastlines around the world. The white areas show which parts of the Earth were covered by permanent ice during the last ice age.

Flooding

If all the water currently stored as ice was to melt, sea levels would rise by about 70 m. Many countries and cities around the world would be underwater.

> During the last ice age, glaciers covered almost one-third of the land on Earth.

Glaciers

Ice in the ice caps is called glacial ice. Water is also stored in glaciers in other places in the world, for example in mountain ranges such as the Himalayas. Glaciers are like very slowly moving frozen rivers. They are so heavy that they can reshape the landscape over hundreds or thousands of years.

Glacier in Torres del Paine national park in Chile

Humans and the Water Cycle

Water is essential to life on Earth. We need fresh water to drink and grow crops. The water cycle creates new fresh water by evaporating water from the oceans and leaving the salt behind. Without the water cycle, humans couldn't survive.

Water consumption

Each person in the UK uses an average of about 150 litres of water a day. The most water-intensive activities are flushing the toilet and showering. If you also count water that is needed to produce our food and household products, we each consume around 3,400 litres per day!

Recycling water

As the human population grows, particularly in cities, it is becoming more and more important to use water sustainably. This is because the water cycle cannot naturally provide enough fresh water in many places. Recycling wastewater through modern water treatment technology is one way of reducing the pressures on the water cycle.

1. Water is used in households and factories.

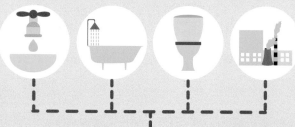

2. Water is treated to remove waste.

3. Treated water can be used for purposes such as irrigation.

Power

Humans harness the water cycle to generate electricity. Dams can be built to collect water and generate hydroelectric power. In 2015, hydropower generated 16.6 per cent of the world's total electricity and 70 per cent of all renewable electricity.

A hydroelectric plant in the Canadian Rocky Mountains

Agriculture

The amount of water needed for farming is about one hundred times the amount of water we use for our personal needs such as drinking and bathing. Because many places don't get enough rain, this demand is often met by drawing water up from wells that use groundwater. This can cause problems in areas where the water cycle cannot replace the groundwater as quickly as it is used. This is an unsustainable use of water.

It takes about 8 litres of seawater to make 4 litres of fresh water.

Desalination

In the future, it is possible that we will rely less on the water cycle to meet our water needs, as desalination technology is developed. This would turn salty seawater into drinkable fresh water. At the moment, however, is too difficult and expensive to be a solution to meet people's water needs.

Glossary

aquifer a layer of underground rock that water can pass through

bedrock the solid base layer of rock underground

contrails the long, thin trails of condensation that aeroplanes leave behind in the sky

convectional rainfall a type of rainfall caused when air is heated by the hot ground, rises upwards, cools, and drops the moisture it was carrying

desalination a process by which the salt is removed from seawater to make fresh drinking water

delta an area of land where a river divides into smaller rivers before it meets the sea

dew point the temperature at which dew starts to form

frontal rainfall a type of rainfall caused when a mass of hot air and a mass of cold air meet

glacier a slowly moving mass of ice

humidity the amount of water vapour in the air

hydroelectric power renewable electricity that is generated by water turning turbines, particularly in large dams

ice cap a large covering of ice over land, particularly near the poles

impermeable does not let water soak into it

infiltration the soaking of water into gaps in the soil and the rock underground

okta a unit of measurement for cloud cover

permeable allows water to soak into it

relief rainfall a type of rainfall that is created when warm air is forced to rise by the landscape, and then cools, dropping the moisture it was carrying

saturated when a cloud or soil cannot hold any more water

stoma a microscopic hole in the leaf of a plant that releases gases; stomata is the plural term

sublimation a process by which ice changes directly to water vapour

subtropical forest a forest that grows in the area of the world bordering the tropics

temperate region an area between the tropics and the poles that is not very hot or very cold

transpiration the process by which water is drawn up through plants and released into the air as water vapour

tributary a small stream or river that feeds into a larger river

updraught an upward current of air

water store where water is held for a period of time before moving on to the next stage of the water cycle

water table the level below which the ground is saturated with water

water vapour water in its gas form

watershed the outer edge of a river basin's catchment area

Test yourself!

1 How much of the Earth's surface is covered by water?

2 Which can hold more water, hot air or cold air?

3 What is transpiration?

4 What type of clouds look like fluffy cotton wool?

5 Rain, sleet, snow and hail are all types of what?

6 What is the name of the dry area behind a hill or mountain range?

7 Name three different water stores.

8 What is the name of the process for removing salt from seawater?

Check your answers on page 32.

Further reading

Water Cycle (Our Earth Series)
Jen Green (Wayland, 2011)

Rivers (Our Earth in Action)
Chris Oxlade (Franklin Watts, 2014)

Water (Earth Cycles)
Sally Morgan (Franklin Watts, 2012)

Websites

Read more about the water cycle at the following websites:

water.usgs.gov/edu/watercycle-kids-adv.html

pmm.nasa.gov/education/water-cycle

www.metoffice.gov.uk/learning/weather-for-kids/water-cycle

Index

Answers

1 71 per cent

2 Hot air

3 The process where water in the ground is sucked up by plants and released into the air as water vapour.

4 Cumulus clouds

5 Precipitation

6 A rain shadow

7 Oceans, rivers, lakes, ponds, ice caps, groundwater, swamps

8 Desalination

GEOGRAPHICS
Series contents lists

Biomes
• What is a Biome? • Forests
• Yosemite • Rainforests • The
Amazon Rainforest • Grasslands
and Savannahs • The Serengeti
• Deserts • The Sahara Desert
• Tundra and Ice • Antarctica
• Oceans • The Great Barrier Reef
• Rivers and Lakes • The Nile River

Earthquakes
• What is an Earthquake?
• Tectonic Plates • Plate Boundaries
and Faults • San Francisco 1906
• Measuring Earthquakes
• Earthquake Hazards • Peru 1970
• Earthquakes and Buildings
• Rescue and Relief • Nepal 2015
• Preparing for Earthquakes
• Tsunamis • Japan 2011

Earth's Resources
• What are Resources? • Mining
• Wood • Plastic • Recycling and
Rubbish • Agriculture • GM Crops
• Fishing • North Sea Fishing
• Recycling • Fossil Fuels
• Sustainable Energy • Eco-cities

Mountains
• What is a Mountain?
• Moving Plates • Fold and Block
Mountains • Volcanic Mountains
• The Andes • Changing Mountains
• The Alps • Climate • Biomes
• The Rocky Mountains • People
and Mountains • The Himalayas
• Mountain Resources
• The Appalachian Mountains

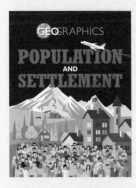

Population and Settlement
• What are Population and
Settlement? • Distribution and
Density • Population Growth
• Overpopulation • Population
Structure • Uganda and Japan
• Migration • UK Migration
• Settlement Sites • Athens
• Settlement Layout • Manila
• Changing Settlements

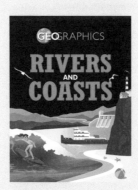

Rivers and Coasts
• Rivers and Coasts • River
Structure • The Ganges River
• River Erosion • River Formations
• The Colorado River • Types of
Coasts • The UK Coast • Changing
Coasts • Arches and Stacks • The
Twelve Apostles • People and
Water • The Three Gorges Dam
• Flooding • Venice

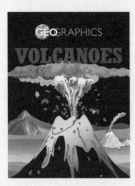

Volcanoes
• What are Volcanoes?
• Formation • The Ring of Fire
• Stratovolcanoes • Mount Fuji
• Shield Volcanoes • Mauna Kea
• Calderas and Cinder Cones
• Eruption • Mount Vesuvius
• Lava • Underwater Volcanoes
• Dormant and Extinct Volcanoes

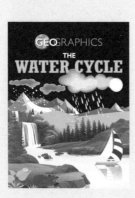

The Water Cycle
• What is the Water Cycle?
• Our Blue Planet • Evaporation
• The Amazon Rainforest
• Condensation • Clouds
• Precipitation • Rainfall • Rain in
the Himalayas • Accumulation
• River Basins • The Mississippi River
• Water Stores • Polar Ice Caps
• Humans and the Water Cycle